Dynamic Learning Styles

Stuart W Macmillan

Copyright©2011 Stuart Macmillan

All rights reserved. No part of this book may be reproduced or used in any form or by any means, electronic or physically, including photocopying, recording, blog, social network or by any information storage or retrieval system or school library without obtaining prior permission in writing from the author. Inquiries should be addressed to the address below.

Published by:
Character Education Programmes of New Zealand (CEPNZ)
PO Box 20-616, Glen Eden, Auckland 0641
New Zealand

www.cepnz.com and www.cepnz.co.nz

ISBN: 978-0-9582903-5-7

CONTENTS

Dynamic Learning Styles

INTRODUCTION

You will probably find quite a few books have been written about Multiple Intelligences and learning styles but through *Dynamic Learning Styles*, our aim is to provide you with straight forward tips and ready-to-use methods.

These are designed to immediately enhance your ability to teach others and techniques that you can apply to your own life long learning process and give to your children or students to help them learn faster and more efficiently.

Learning Styles:

Some writers try to complicate matters by introducing such a long list of learning styles that that boundaries between each one are hard to identify or at least, they would be very hard to cater to the needs of each individual style. Some even go further to complicate matters by calling them "Multiple Intelligences".

From here on in, this book is written as if you are the teacher and lessons are given for students also but anyone can use the guidelines of this book to either teach or learn for themselves.

In this book, we do not want to put down the theories or research that has taken place in this field but merely simplify matters to make education fun and fulfilling for both the teacher and the pupil.

In *Dynamic Learning Styles* we emphasis the learning styles that come naturally through the five senses.

These are:

- Sight - visually learning by what is seen.
- Hearing - auditory learning by what one hears.
- Touch - learning through doing things, experience and emotional feelings.
- Smell – the association of smells with what is being learnt and information.
- Taste – the association of tastes with information.

Each of the five senses can be used and combined to make learning more effective. You will also find that each person may react differently to the style of teaching that is being used as each student will learn more effectively according to their personal learning style.

This means that if, for example, a student learns better through a "hands-on" approach, he or she may not learn as easily through the "theory" part of the lessons. The same applies to a student that learns best by reading about something. This type of student may not pick things up as well if they are read to aloud.

Therefore, as a teacher, you will need to identify the preferred learning style of each of your students and teach in order to satisfy these requirements.

Stuart Macmillan

DISCOVERING THE LEARNING STYLES OF YOUR STUDENTS

In order to be able to teach to students in a manner that they will best be able to learn, you need to discover what their learning style is. Before we look at some ways in testing your students to find this out, let's take a look at a way in which you can find out how they process the information you are giving them in order to make your first discovery of their learning style.

Have you ever heard that expression "they eyes are the windows to the soul"? There may be some truth in this as you can find out how a person processes information by watching their eye movements. These eye movements can also tell you what their best learning style is. Let's take a look...

Although we have previously states that learning happens through each of the five senses, these can be further reduced to three main categories:

1. Visual (learning by watching, reading and seeing)

2. Auditory (learning through listening and hearing)

3. Kinesthetic (learning by physically doing things - "hands-on" approach)

Just by looking at people's eyes when you ask them questions or talk to them, you can get an instant appraisal of their learning style and how they are processing information in their brain. The examples on the next page are for regular right handed people.

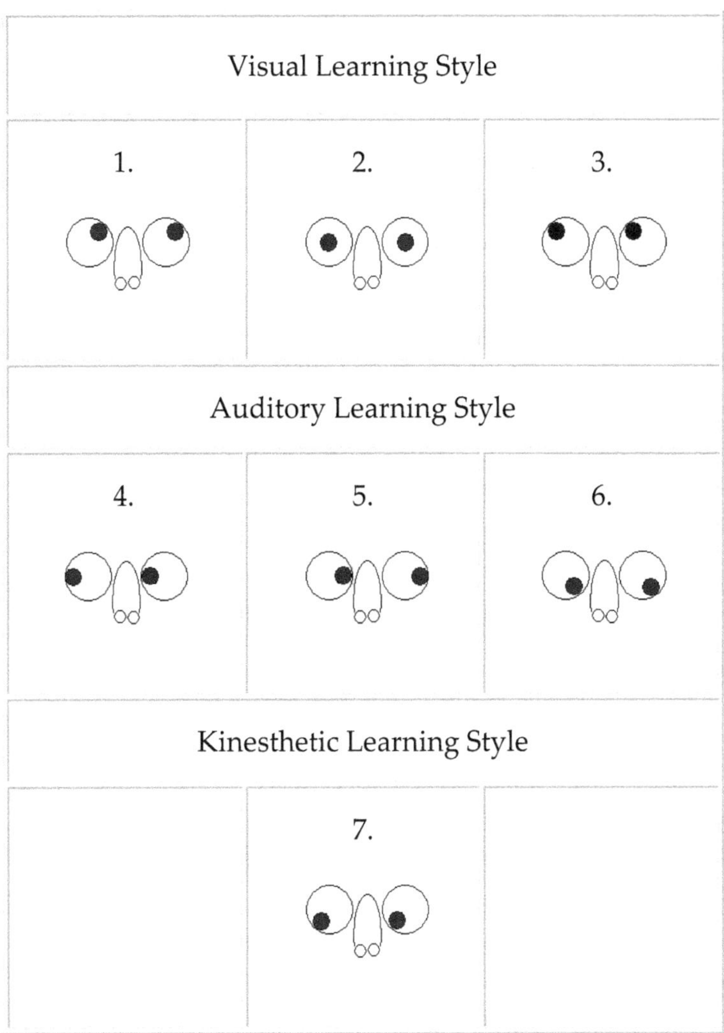

Visual Learning Style

1.

2.

3.

Auditory Learning Style

4.

5.

6.

Kinesthetic Learning Style

7.

Have you ever noticed that when you ask a question of someone or even enquire about how a persons holiday was, more often than not, they will move their eyes around in one direction or another. This shows you how the person is recalling the information they are talking about.

If they move their eyes upward and to the left or right or look straight ahead as if looking into the distance, they are trying to visualise the answer to the question or remember a picture they have in their head.

If they move their eyes straight toward the left or right or look down and to the left, they are trying to remember what they heard that relates to the question or remember a sound they have in their head (often the voice of the person that gave them the answer in the first place).

If the person looks down and to the right they are recalling actually doing something. It could be writing or building something or the physical sensations associated (temperature, comfortability, taste, pain or pleasure) with what is being recalled.

Remember, you need to know if the person is left or right handed first in order for this to be successful.

Try this out now. Remember the position of the eyes when you talk to others and you can turn a mundane conversation into something more challenging and rewarding.

Discovering the Truth:

People who master these techniques of discovering persons thinking processes can also find out if the person is telling the truth or lying! Imagine the progress you could make in conflict resolution.

Let's take it a little further:

In image 3 the person is looking up and to the right. Although associated with visual recall, the person is trying to visually construct something they have not seen before. Whereas in image 1 the person in recalling something them have actually seen.

In image 4 the person is to the right. Although associated with auditory recall, the person is trying to construct a sound or phrase that they have not heard before. Whereas in image 5 the person in recalling something them have actually heard and in image 6, they are talking to themselves.

In Kinesthetic processing, image 7, the person is trying to recall feelings.

So, from this you will not only be able to find out how your students learn but also how truthful a person is actually being with you. For example, the answer to the simple question "Did you watch the news last night for your assignment?" could be analysed by watching the eye movement. If the person looks up and/or to the right, they are constructing an answer based on imagination. In other words...no they didn't watch the news (if they are right handed remember!).

CATERING FOR ALL STYLES OF LEARNING

Now that you understand about learning styles, how can you ensure that you cater for each style when your class of students is made up of a variation of styles? This is how you can make your classes more interesting and make learning a fun thing for your students, no matter what age they are.

Let's begin:

We already know that some students will react better to different styles of teaching so how can you cater to all at once?

During each class, it is important to implement elements that will emphasise the message being given through each learning style. To do this you need to use techniques that will invoke the receptiveness of the learning style of each of the students.

Techniques:

The bulk of your class will react favourably to both audio and visual presentation of the lesson. Even without technological assistance, the way in which you present yourself, speak and act in front of the class can act as a catalyst to learning.

Here are some pointers:

- Vary the pitch and volume of your voice throughout the lessons. This will "wake up" many of your students and will instantly invoke the learning style of those students that learn best through listening and increase the attention of the other learning styles. In the 1970's it was actually been proven by Bulgarian educator and psychologist, Dr. Georgi Lozanov that rhythmic variation in the tone of the teachers voice (from normal to soft and then loud) can increase the students ability to learn material being taught.

- In the same stance, use noises to attract the attention of the class. Slap a ruler onto the table or emphasis a point with a clap of the hands (yours and/or theirs).

Note: Points of the lesson that are important to remember can be more easily recalled by you students at a future time if the point is emphasised in conjunction with a noise (a clap, a ringing bell, etc). Every time that the same point is raised, use the same noise in conjunction and tell the students to remember the particular noise as they write it down or each time the point is mentioned. It could be a good idea to use a tape recorder to record some unusual sounds or store some on your laptop or on a CD for instant access at the required time (you can download many for free from the Internet).

- Use props to attract the attention of the visual learners. This can be any object from a costume, hat or scarf to an apple, ball, musical instrument, torch, or anything unusual you may find on your visits to garage sales or "op-shops". It does not matter if the object is not relevant to the lesson. In fact, the more obscure or unrelated the object is, the more interested the class will be.

- Take a look at the "Train Your Brain to Focus and Learn" section of the students page "Removing Distractions". In conjunction with this exercise it is a good idea to introduce a "sound" to enhance the memory of the excited state of the students produced to enhance their learning ability through focus. A good idea would be to ring a small bell when this state has been reached. Do this at the beginning of each class as the exercise is being practiced. Then, once the students have done this for a week or so, all you will need to do, to save time, is ring the small bell and you will have the students undivided attention. Try it. This has been proven to work!

- Introduce background music to your class while you are teaching or while the students are studying. It has been proven that the majority of people can learn easier if their mind is stimulated by ambient music or music that is set to a particular tempo. Baroque music often provides the best results especially Baroque concertos of the 17th and 18th century by composers such as Vivaldi, Corelli, Handel and Bach or any soothing or peaceful music at 60 beats per minute (often listed as *largo* - ask your music department). If you decide to use music in your class, do NOT use "heavy-metal" or "hip-hop" or any other type of "modern" music unless you are teaching physical education, dance or drama. Popular music tends to stay in the fore-front of the mind and can even distract a person from learning. If you don't have any music available, another 'prop' that can achieve the same results is a metronome set at 60 beats per minute (this was proven by two American doctors in the 1950s - Linn Cooper and Milton Erickson).

- When you ask your students to complete an assignment, give them alternatives on how they can present these assignments - a visual or graphic presentation, a speech, a written report, a short play conducted with a couple of other students, a survey. This way, you will be encouraging them to find the best style that they can learn by and correlate information. As a teacher, you will also discover the pupils best leaning style.

- Introduce new subject matter through an open discussion or group activity. Have them solve problems through team work and combine their input into a presentation. One can draw the illustrations, another does the writing and another presents the combined information to the class. Advanced classes could work together on a PowerPoint (or similar) presentation on their computers.

- If the class is appropriate, the subject being studied could be acted out in a role-play or you could take your class on a field trip for hands-on experience using all their five senses.

KEEPING THE ATTENTION OF YOUR CLASS

Before you begin your class and implement one or more of the above practices, it is best to create the right state of mind in your students to make them even more receptive to what you are about to teach them.

Before you start the class, ask each student to try and remember the last time they were successful at something - anything. Tell them to visualise this event in their mind and try and remember all the facts and feeling that surrounded that success - the way they felt inside and out (joyful, happy, proud, tired, hungry, muddy); what was the weather like at the time (sunny, warm, cold, windy); can they picture the faces of people that were around you when you had your success (or shared in it); were there any distinctive smells in the air at the time?; what time was it...of day, of the week, of the year?; try to remember, feel and picture in your head everything that surrounded that success.

In this fashion, you are creating in the mind of your students all the facets that they associate with the feeling of success. This will induce the state of mind of feeling as successful as they did in the past and therefore open their mind to be more successful and remember all that they are studying. This is the right and best state for learning anything, even if it is totally unrelated to the subject being taught and is a great state to be in if they are sitting an exam.

The use of one of more of the techniques listed above can enhance the students ability to stay tuned to what you are teaching them. In order to ensure that the students remain focussed, you also have to address each of the students learning styles as you speak.

The structure of your sentences and questioning will act as a catalyst to stimulate each students particular learning style. Use phrases such as "Do you see what I mean by...?", "Can you picture...?", "Can you grasp what I mean...?", "Does that ring any bells?", "Can you imagine...?", "Can you picture the last time...?", "Do you remember the last time I told you...?", "What would it look like if...?", "Can you imagine what it would feel like...?", "If you could ask a question of...what would it be?".

Adopting this line of questioning while you are teaching will invoke each of the different styles of learning in your students through their senses. This will make them active or **dynamic** learners in every class and in every subject.

At the same time, listen to the responses that you get from your students, the words that they use in their questions as applicable to the phrases used in the structure of your sentences mentioned above. Listen for key words that will tell you their learning style (remember...see, picture, hear, tell, feel, grasp).

Through these methods, your students WILL learn easier and be able to remember what they have learnt through the recall of the imagination and sensory stimulation used in the classroom.

Then, you will be a *Dynamic* Teacher.

Stuart Macmillan

HOW YOU LEARN

Before you can find out how to learn things easier, you need to know how you actually learn.

If you are in a classroom or learning by yourself, facts are being put to your mind in many different ways through all of your senses.

For example: When you are watching television, facts are being put into your brain through the senses of sight (the pictures you are watching) and hearing (the sounds going with the pictures). If you were watching a sports game that you are really interested in, you will also get facts through your feelings like the excitement of a player scoring a goal.

But is this really learning? Yes, everything that happens around you affects you in one way or another and this information (the facts) is stored in your brain...it is being learnt. This information can be brought out from your brain at any time in the future.

Have you ever had that feeling of smelling something in the air that brings on a memory from some time ago? Maybe you hear something being said that makes you remember hearing it before? These are examples of remembering something that you have learnt that has been stored in your brain and this could have happened without you even knowing you were doing it.

From this we can see that you learn through:

- Sight - everything you see through reading and watching.
- Sound - everything you hear.
- Smell - everything you smell (stinky or nice).
- Taste - you learn easily about things you like or do not like to eat or taste.
- Touch - from doing or making things with your hands.

These ways that you learn can also be made greater by the way you act to the information your brain gets and can also be made bigger through a mix of more than one sense at a time.

For example: Let's say that you are served a plate of food that you haven't tasted before. First of all, you don't like the smell of the food. Next, it isn't very nice to look at. Then you pick it up with your fingers and it doesn't feel very nice and put some in your mouth and it tastes nasty. All this is mixed in your brain and you label it with a feeling of dislike.

The next time you smell the same smell of that food or see it, you remember that same feeling of dislike and maybe even the taste of it and you will not want it.

By this bad experience you have learnt something. The same happened when you were younger and you touched something that was very hot. You certainly wouldn't do that again! You have learnt a lesson from the past.

So far, we have looked at the way that your brain learns for itself, now let's take a look at ways in which you learn when you are wanting to learn.

In the Classroom:

In the classroom you are sitting with other students at desks and a teacher is standing at the front of the class. It is the teachers role to teach you all that you need to know in order to learn what you are studying.

As a student, it is your task to pay attention to the teacher and listen to all that you are told and do all the work that the teacher gives you to do.

All this, you know already but what is happening in the classroom?

As the teacher speaks, you are listening. If your mind drifts off onto something else like what you are going to do when you get home or you start looking out the window, you may miss something and wonder why the class laughs when you ask a question about something that has already been said...so...pay attention at all times!

As you are listening, it is a good idea to take notes on things that you feel could be of use in future study. If the teacher writes something on the board, take a note of it.

In this example, you have used three ways of learning:

1. You have listened

2. You have watched

3. You have acted (taking notes)

This is just the same as when you were watching that great film on TV. If you can remember a film you have watched and talk about it with your friends later, you can use the same ways to remember your school lessons and remember them later on.

To find out how you can get better at the way that you learn and remember more, go on to the next page: Find your best way to learn.

Stuart Macmillan

FIND YOUR BEST WAY TO LEARN

In the last chapter, you learnt about how you learn using all of your senses. Now you will now find out the best way to help you learn better and faster.

Every person has a different way in which they learn things. These ways are learning by Looking, Hearing and Touching. Let's take a look at how this relates to you and find out what type you would be and then how you can best use this.

Looking – Hearing – Touching

A simple test can be got from your teacher on how you can find out which learning style you fit into. Follow through the *"Discover Your Learning Style"* test in the next chapter.

While you are waiting for that test you can go through the list below and find out for yourself.

"Looking" Learning Style:

If you are a "Looking" learner, these are things you might do...

Firstly, you will be using sentences such as "I see what you mean", "I can't quite picture that", "Can you imaging..." and "Is that clear to you?". Your sentences will be made up with words that have something to do with sight, seeing things and pictures.

You will also...like people to look at you when you are talking to them; sit near the front of the class; do well on tests where you have to read a lot; do good with maths by picturing it in your head; like maps and pictures to show you how to get somewhere; spell words easier by seeing the word in your head with your eyes closed; write a lot of notes to help you learn.

"Hearing" Learning Style:

If you are a "Hearing" learner, these are things you might do...

Firstly, you will be using sentences such as "That sounds good", "I hear what you're saying", "what do think about..." and "Listen to what I have to say". Your sentences will be made up with words that have something to do with sound or hearing.

You will also...sit in class when you can hear well but do not need to see what is going on; like people telling you about things instead of reading it for yourself; say out words and numbers when spelling or adding; be put off by sounds around you; like to talk to other people about things; talk out loud to yourself at times; learn easier by reading aloud; learn easier if you listen to what is being said.

"Touching" Learning Style:

If you are a "Touching" learner, these are things you might do...

Firstly, you will be using sentences such as "I can't quite get hold of what you are talking about", "How do you feel about...", and "Get in touch with me". Your sentences will be made up with words that have something to do with feelings, touch, or holding.

You will also...sit in the class where you can get up of move around; like to write things down as you learn them; draw pictures to help you learn things; will do well when you have a chance to use your hands to do something for yourself or make something; spell better by writing the word out and seeing if it 'feels' right.

This list is not full and each person may be different in some ways and you may also find that you can learn in lots of different ways. After you have done the 'learning styles test' from your teacher and found out your best learning style, you may find it a good idea to do things using to ways above...you may be surprised by how much more you can learn!

DISCOVER YOUR LEARNING STYLE

For each of these questions, circle the letter for the first answer that comes into your head (A, B or C). There are no right or wrong answers so don't spend much time thinking about if your answer is right.

1. When you study, what would you rather do:

    A. Read notes, read a book or look at pictures or diagrams that relate to the topic?

    B. Have someone ask you questions and see if you can answer them, or repeat facts silently to yourself?

    C. Write things out on study cards and make models or draw diagrams?

2. When you are asked to spell a word, which would you do:

    A. Picture it in your head?

    B. Sound the word out and spell it in your head?

    C. Write it down first and see if it 'feels' right?

3. What kind of classroom would you rather NOT study in:

    A. Where the lighting is too bright or it is very sunny?

    B. Where there are too many noises around you or other people talking?

    C. Where the seats are uncomfortable?

4. When you listen to music, which of these things do you do most of the time:

    A. Daydream or do other things while you listen?

    B. Sing or hum along to the music?

    C. Tap your foot or move with the timing?

5. When you work at solving a problem do you:

    A. Make a list and check off each of the items as you do them?

    B. Talk to friends or others about it?

    C. Draw a picture of the problem or picture each of the steps in your mind?

6. When you read for fun, which of these would you prefer:

    A. A book with lots of pictures in it?

    B. A book with lots of characters and conversations in it?

    C. A role playing adventure book where you answer questions and solve riddles?

7. To learn how a machine works, would you rather:

   A. Read the instruction manual and look at the diagrams?
   B. Have someone explain it to you?
   C. Have a look at the real thing yourself and maybe take it apart?

8. If you were given three choices to pass you time, which one would you want to do:

   A. Draw pictures?
   B. Listen to music?
   C. Go for a run?

9. If you were given three choices on how to do a project, would you rather:

   A. Write about it?
   B. Turn it into a speech?
   C. Create a role-play about it?

10. If your teacher had to leave the room and you weren't ask to study by yourself, what would you most likely do:

   A. Look out the window or around the class?
   B. Talk to someone sitting near you?
   C. Get out of your chair or move around in your chair?

THINKING OUTSIDE THE SQUARE

This is something that may help you to learn more on any subject you are being taught.

If you were to call the subject matter you are being taught the "square", then "thinking outside the square" means to look at all other possibilities, options and related topics in connection to the matter being studied or taught.

Let's look at an example. Say you are in biology and you are studying the heart. The "heart" is the "square" you are studying. In order to fully learn about the heart, you should also find out more about all the topics that surround this subject in order to fully understand it and learn what you are being taught. Take a look at the diagram on the next page:

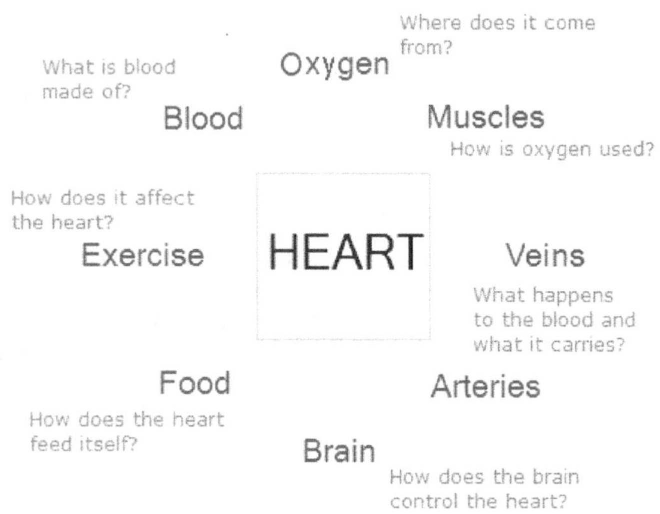

What you are building up is a cross-reference for all the topics that could possibly relate to the heart to give you greater knowledge. When you go on to study, for example the lungs, you would have already "thought outside the square" by learning about where the blood obtains the oxygen content it carries and what happens to it as it goes throughout the body being used by tissues, muscles and organs through the arteries and veins.

With your cross-reference to exercise, you can monitor your own pulse rate and see what happens to it as you walk and compare it to after you have gone for a run. You will also be able to understand why it is that your muscles can ache a bit after long stretches of activity - perhaps there is not enough "food" (oxygen) getting to the muscles so you have to learn to breathe more efficiently to ensure that the right amount of required oxygen is getting to your muscles. When you think about the heart in such a manner, you will easily recall these "outside" topics in a test that will help you to remember.

It doesn't matter what topic you are studying. The more that you look outside the square of the basic subject, the more you will find it easier to understand the topic and easily pick up on the related topics as you study them.

Take a look...

You are baking bread in a cooking class: Where does flour come from? What exactly is yeast? What does temperature do to the process at the different stages? How do different types of bread taste? Why does it grow mould after a while?

You are studying algebra in your Mathematics class: How did the idea of algebra originate? What famous people used it and why? What types of people use it in their day to day work? (with this question, don't say to yourself, "well I'm not going to be doing that when I leave school". All you are doing is becoming more aware of its uses in order to learn outside the square and make it more interesting) Why do we use letters instead of numbers? Can you get the same results if you put the equation back to front? Can you present the same answer with a different equation?

You are studying Hamlet in you English class: Who are all the characters and how are they related? What was the world like and how did people live in the days that the play is set? What do the stage directions mean? What sort of accent do you think the people of Denmark would have if they spoke English? If you lived in that setting, how do you think you would cope? Which character do you best relate to?

As you can see, you can make whatever subject or topic you are study become more interesting and meaningful just by digging a little deeper and thinking outside the square. Keep this up and when it comes to a test, you WILL remember things easier.

REMOVING DISTRACTIONS

The opposite to "Removing Distractions" is increasing attention. These are several way in which you can do both at the same time.

First, you really need to know what attention is and what you should be putting your attention on. How many times have you heard that phrase "Pay attention"? Needless to say, if you are being distracted from what you are supposed to be learning or doing, this has been said to you.

The Online Wikipedia definition of attention is..."the cognitive process of selectively concentrating on one thing while ignoring other things. Examples include listening carefully to what someone is saying while ignoring other conversations in the room."

In other words, attention is the ability to concentrate on one thing while ignoring other things (distractions).

You can you remove these distractions and increase your attention in a number of ways.

First, you need to find a "focus". Have you ever used a magnifying glass to burn something on a sunny day? You moved the magnifying glass back and forth until the image of the sun through the glass was the smallest. This meant that all the suns rays were "focussed" onto one point, magnifying the energy of those rays. Only then did you get results.

The same applies to your mind and increasing your learning ability. Have you ever had that experience when you were deep into a TV programme and someone said something to you from across the room? Your mind would have registered that you hear someone say something but because you full attention was "focussed" on the TV, you didn't really hear what was said...it was muffled as a sound in the background. You could have chosen to ignore that 'sound' and continue with your attention on the TV or broken your focus and asked, "Sorry, what was that?"

If you could apply that same "focus" (as in the magnifying glass or the TV viewing) in the classroom or while you are studying, your ability to learn would vastly improve!

When you get into a classroom (or you are doing homework at home), you first need to get all the distractions put out of your mind. Sit down, make yourself comfortable, ignore any chit-chat that may be going on around your and then concentrate on your focus...today you are going to learn something you never want to forget and it is going to be exciting! Nothing is going to distract me!

The best way to increase your focus and ignore distractions, as just pointed out, is to increase your brains desire to learn. How do you tell your brain that it (and of course you) want to learn?

Train Your Brain to Focus and Learn:

Think of a time in the past where you were very excited, eager, happy and your mind was on one thing only. An example of this could be one time at Christmas when you were very young and you were staring at the presents beneath the tree waiting eagerly until the time that you could open them. Another could be a time when you were sitting in the cinema waiting for a movie to start that you have been very eager and excited about seeing.

What you are looking for is the experience and feelings before hand and NOT the actual opening of the present or the watching of the movie.

When you have thought of that time, think and remember everything about that moment. What could you smell in the air (popcorn, dinner cooking, fresh pine needles, etc)? What was the temperature where you were? How did your body feel (tingling with excitement, warm, alert, sweating, mouth watering, etc)? How fast do you think your pulse was racing in the excitement? Think of everything that affected your five senses of sight, sound, smell, taste and feelings.

Every single point that you can remember will help you to actually start feeling those same feelings again. While you are in that same state of mind as you were at that exciting time, say to yourself, "I am about to learn something I never want to forget and it is going to be exciting! Nothing is going to distract me!" and at the same time, pinch yourself on the arm!

If you repeat this same exercise every time a class is about to begin, within a week, all you will need to do is pinch yourself on the arm and you will instantly be in the same state of mind -

one of eagerness and full focus on what you are about to learn. You will be able to absorb more information that you have ever done before and ignore any distractions that may occur inside the classroom or outside the window!

Stuart Macmillan

IMPROVING YOUR MEMORY

"I just can't remember!" Have you ever said that to yourself or to someone else? I think we all have!

The fact is that we all have a brain and whatever happens in our lives, whoever we meet, whatever we say or do or what ever we learn, is always kept inside our brain despite the fact that we may not be able to recall it at that moment.

The reason why you are unable to remember even the simplest of things (at times) is because you did not pay attention or focus on the information or event to be remembered at the time that you first saw it or the event took place.

Try this...can you remember what you had for dinner for each of the last 7 days? Or...can you remember what colour your towel is in your bathroom? How about this one...can you remember what time of the week you favourite programme is on TV? Or...do you know what date the next school holidays start?

Can you see the difference in your ability to remember? Things that seem trivial are harder to remember than things that you WANT to remember. Therefore if you want to remember things that you learn in class, you need to pay more attention and focus on what you are learning. School may seem boring or trivial at times but it is up to you to change it so that you find it more interesting by taking advantage of your learning style and making each class more fun and interesting.

Further on in this section you will learn some fun ways to help you remember things, but for now, let's look at your memory and how you can improve it.

Definition (from Wikipedia, the free online encyclopedia): "Memory is the ability of an organism to store, retain, and subsequently recall information."

So, memory involves storing, keeping and recalling things. You can look at this like a computer: information is put into the computer as input (storing) and is kept in its memory (keeping) and when you want the information again from the computers memory, it is described as output (recalling).

The same happens with your brain so you have to train it to store, keep and recall in the best possible way. Let's take a look at some ways in which you can store information better:

1. In the section "Train Your Brain to Focus and Learn", you learnt a very good method of ensuring that you keep your focus on what you are learning. This is called motivating yourself to learn. When you are motivated, you will easily store the information in your brain in such a way as to make it easier to remember.

2. Ignore any distractions and keep your mind focussed on what you are trying to learn.

3. Relax yourself. Don't go to sleep though! When you are relaxed and you are not thinking about other things at home or around the school, you will learn better.

4. Use your imagination. You can use many different ways to remember things through your imagination. If you are reading a book for class, imagine that you are there in the setting. What is going on around you? Try to picture all the descriptive scenes in your minds eye. Imagine yourself as one of the characters. If you make the book more interesting to yourself through your imagination, you will remember more.

5. Always keep in mind your learning style. If you use this effectively you will be

giving information to your brain in the way that it wants to receive it. This way your brain will more readily accept the information as if it is its favourite food and you will remember it later.

6. If you are still unsure of your preferred learning style, use all of your senses every time you receive information in class or at home. Don't just look at it, draw it, write it, say it out loud or to yourself, listen to it, feel the way that it sounds. It doesn't matter what the information is, you can process it in the same way.

$a^2 + b^2 = c^2$ ... How do your lips move when you say it? Look in the mirror...as you say it, does it look like you are grinning by the time you say the letter "c"? What 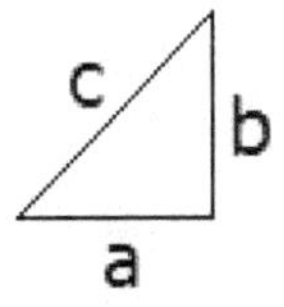 type of sound are you making as you say each letter? Can you see a triangle in your head with the letters in the right place for this equation? Can you see (c) the hippopotamus climbing up the longest side of the triangle (Hypotenuse)?

7. After the end of a days learning, review all the things you studied during that day before you go to bed and once again when you get up and are getting dressed the next morning. Make this a habit and you will find that your brain will file away the information as important as you

sleep and you will recall it the next morning with ease. Remember, habits take some time to become habits (second nature) so you need to make yourself do this for at least a week and then you will see results.

If you combine all of these methods while you are learning, you WILL remember things easier in the future.

Here are some fun ways to help you remember things:

Mnemonics (pronounced "ne-mon-ics" with the stress on the "mon")

Definition (from Wikipedia, the free online encyclopedia):

"Mnemonics are memory aids. Mnemonics are often verbal, something such as a very short poem or a special word used to help a person remember something, particularly lists. Mnemonics rely not only on repetition to remember facts, but also on associations between easy-to-remember constructs and lists of data, based on the principle that the human mind much more easily remembers data attached to spatial, personal or otherwise meaningful information than that occurring in meaningless sequences. The sequences must make sense though.

The major assumption is that there are two sorts of memory: the "natural" memory and the "artificial" memory. The former is inborn, and is the one that everyone uses every day. The artificial memory is one that is trained through learning and practicing a variety of mnemonic techniques. The latter can be used to perform feats of memory that are quite extraordinary, impossible to carry out using the natural memory alone."

Starting on the next page are some examples of mnemonics that you can use:

The number of days in each month of the year:

> Thirty days has September,
>
> April, June, and November;
>
> All the rest have thirty-one,
>
> Excepting February alone,
>
> Which has but twenty-eight, in line,
>
> Till Leap Year gives it twenty-nine.

The order of the planets from the sun:

> "**So My Very Eager Mother Just Served Us Nine Pizzas**"

> Sun, Mercury, Venus, Earth, Mars, Jupiter, Saturn, Uranus, Neptune, Pluto

---

Colours of the Rainbow in the order of the spectrum:

Roy G. Biv or "**R**ainbows **O**n **Y**our **G**lass **B**rings **I**nstant **V**ision"

(Red, Orange, Yellow, Green, Blue, Indigo, Violet).

Points of the compass in a clockwise direction:

Noisy **E**ngines **S**ound **W**orst:

North, East, South, West

Mnemonics can be fun and make things much easier to remember. You can try and make up your own and this way they will be even easier for you to remember, especially is you make them funny. They can be used in just about every situation and subject matter.

Another style of mnemonics put forward by

John Sambrook in the 1870's was where each number is associated to a word that sounds the same or similar as in the examples below:

1. - Gun, fun, run, son.

2. - Shoe, loo, flu

3. - Tree, knee, see

4. - Door, floor, more

5. - Hive, live, strive

6. - Sticks, licks, kicks

7. - Heaven, raven, leaven

8. - Gate, late, rate

9. - Wine, vine, line

10. - Hen, den, men

Using Sambrook's method, these numbers and words could be used in a "hook and peg" system to develop a little story to make it easier to remember lists of items or numbers.

As an example of the "hook and peg" system, if the word in a list to be remembered was 'bulb' (the hook), the number ONE could be associated to it (the peg to put the hook on) by picturing a GUN shooting out a light BULB. If the word to remember was CARPET, you could 'hook' this onto the FOUR 'peg' by associating the word DOOR with it: I had to open the DOOR before I could see the CARPET.

This can also be a fun system to use to help you learn to remember things.

With each of these methods, you will be able to help yourself to learn much easier, whatever your learning style may be.

Recalling Material During a Test

The best way to recall information during a test is to make sure that you have learnt it correctly in the first place. This means using all of the methods mentioned above.

When you have properly stored the information into your brain in the fun and interesting way that you brain wants to receive it, all you need to do is to remember the way in which the information was stored.

Before you begin the test, take a few deep and slow breaths. Relax yourself and be calm. Keep your eye on the goal of completing the test in the knowledge that you will complete it to the best of your ability. Tell yourself this.

Remember your learning style and go through the senses that you were using while you were learning. Remember the excited state of mind that you created before each class. Did you write the information you are trying to recall? Did you draw a picture? Can you remember the way in which your teacher spoke about it? Can you feel what the setting was like in the class? Did you make up a poem, song, rhyme or mnemonic to remember something?

When you do all this, the information will flow back to you. Let it come naturally and do not try to force the information out of your brain. If you get stuck on a question, it is only a temporary thing. Move onto the next question and come back to that one later...you never know, when you answer the next question or two, they may trigger the memory of the answer to the question you will go back to.

Homework techniques

Everyone has to do homework, it is a fact of school life. Therefore, in order to get your homework done and on time, you need to set yourself some ways to get it done effectively.

The first thing to do is to try and find a place at home where you can concentrate on your homework without distractions. Never have the TV on in front of you or your favourite music playing. These will definitely cause a distraction and you will not learn effectively.

Once you have found your spot (preferably in your own room), make sure you are comfortable and there is plenty of fresh air and lighting.

Whatever the subject may be that you need to study, the book chapter you need to read or the home study questions you need to answer, remember you personal learning style and use each of the methods described on how to use it efficiently. Sight, Sound, Feeling...use them all in your homework as well...take notes, draw pictures, diagrams and charts, say things out loud, make up your own mnemonics or rhymes, if you are an auditory (sound) learner, get someone else to ask you questions on the subject.

When you have finished your homework, you might like to ask one of your parents to take a look at it. The added praise will help you to stay on track.

Most importantly, as mentioned at the beginning of this topic, homework HAS TO BE DONE so make sure you set a start and a finish time to get it done and make this a firm habit.

The best time is as soon as you get home and then it is out of the way.

Be happy while you study...it is not really a "chore" but it is the beginning of the life-long process of learning. If you make it fun and get it done, you will reach your goals and avoid those holes.

Stuart Macmillan

OTHER TITLES BY
STUART MACMILLAN

Teachers
Coach
Stuart Macmillan
and
Elizabeth Macmillan

TEACHERS COACH

(co-authored with Elizabeth Macmillan)

Providing teachers with a refreshing look at teaching skills and guidelines to fundamental qualities to enrich the teaching and administration processes.

Available in paperback and ebook through our website:

www.cepnz.co.nz/coach.html

BULLYING
ELIMINATION
HANDBOOK
THE COMPLETE GUIDE ON HOW TO ELIMINATE
AND PREVENT ALL FORMS OF BULLYING
STUART MACMILLAN

BULLYING ELIMINATION HANDBOOK

THE COMPLETE GUIDE ON HOW TO ELIMINATE AND PREVENT ALL FORMS OF BULLYING.

The bullying elimination handbook shows schools how to implement strategies that reflect a zero-tolerance to bullying. This book and resource kit will provide teachers with what they need to eliminate all forms of bullying from within the school and your local community.

It also includes additional resources that can be downloaded from our website at no additional cost. Once you purchase the book you will find instructions on how to download these resources. If you can not download, we can email them to you at no extra cost.

Available in paperback or E-Book from:

http://www.cepnz.co.nz/bullying.html

Stuart Macmillan

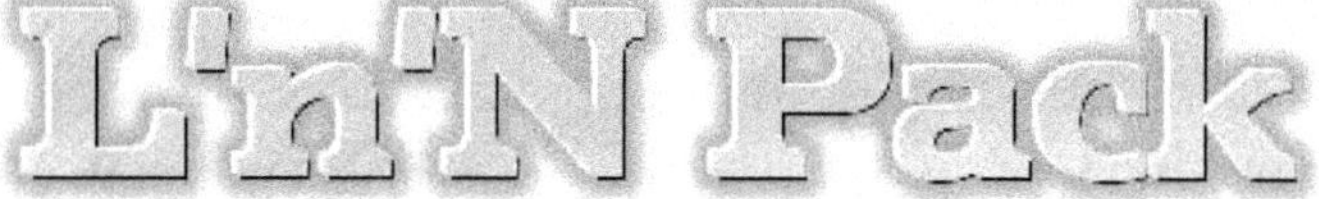

LITERACY & NUMERACY PACK

The Literacy & Numeracy Pack has all your basic Mathematics and English needs in one place. Not only will this provide you with all you need to know to get on in general life but you will also learn methods to remember things, get on with others better, apply for a job and how to easily perform calculations in your head. Great for the everyday needs of adults and students of all ages.

Available as a E-Book from:

http://tinyurl.com/4ulqljj

On CD-ROM from:

http://www.cepnz.co.nz/litnum.html

Being Ardent
About Life
Your Guide to living a
more successful
and fulfilling life
By Stuart Macmillan

BEING ARDENT ABOUT LIFE

Being Ardent about Life teaches you how to implement the ARDENT personal development programme into your life. You will be shown how to take a closer look at your life, develop and understand your values system, set goals, succeed and enjoy life to its fullest.

"The essential guide to enthusiastically living a passionate, successful, happy and fulfilling life!"

"Change your life for the better in time that it takes to read this book!"

Available in paperback and ebook through our website:

www.beingardent.com

Character Education Programmes

of New Zealand (CEPNZ)

For further insights, books and resources see our
website at:

www.cepnz.com

Follow us on social networks for updates and
specials:
Twitter: http://twitter.com/cepnz
Blog: http://blog.cepnz.co.nz/
Facebook: http://facebook.com/schoolkits

www.ingramcontent.com/pod-product-compliance
Lightning Source LLC
Chambersburg PA
CBHW061046050726
47592CB00004B/1612